REVOL
LEADERSHIP

<u>A WORKBOOK</u>

For

DARE TO LEAD

BRENÉ BROWN, Ph.D., LMSW

By

Native-Hub Reads

Table of Contents

HOW TO USE THIS WORKBOOK FOR ENHANCE APPLICATION   5

AUTHOR'S NOTE   6

IT'S NOT THE CRITIC WHO COUNTS   7

INTRODUCTION: MY ADVENTURES IN THE ARENA   9

INTRODUCTION ANALYSIS   20

PART ONE

CHAPTER ONE   22

THE MOMENTS AND THE MYTHS   23

CHAPTER ANALYSIS   34

CHAPTER TWO: 37

THE POWER AND WISDOM TO SERVER OTHERS   38

CHAPTER ANALYSIS   41

CHAPTER THREE: 44

THE AVORY   44

ARMOURED LEADERSHIP VS DARING LEADERSHIP   46

CHAPTER ANALYSIS   49

CHAPTER FOUR   51

SHAME AND EMPATHY   51

EMPATHY   54

WHAT EMPATHY LOOKS LIKE   58

CHAPTER ANALYSIS   64

CHAPTER FIVE   66

WHO WE ARE IS HOW WE LEAD   66

DRIVING GREATNESS FROM CURIOSITY AND LEARNING   68

CHAPTER ANALYSIS   71

PART TWO

CHAPTER SIX   74

CHAPTER ANALYSIS   87

PART THREE

CHAPTER SEVEN   90

CHAPTER ANALYSIS   95

PART FOUR

CHAPTER EIGHT   98

LEARNING TO RISE   99

THE RECKONING   100

THE DELTA   105

CHAPTER ANALYSIS   107

CONCLUSION   110

HOW TO USE THIS WORKBOOK FOR ENHANCE APPLICATION

It's safe to say that life is a circle of learning and that we learn every day. However, some people take the time to make complex subjects easier for us all to understand b y breaking them down to simple and relatable terms. This is exactly what Brené Brown did with her book daring to lead. In the same way, we have written this workbook in such a way that it will help those familiar and those unfamiliar with the book to learn major lessons and get helpful summaries from this book.

There is a singularity of purpose from both authors and that is to help complete beginners in the application of these powerful life changing lessons contained in the book. However, it is of great importance that the reader approaches this book with open mindedness in other to fully grasp the author's message and at the same time, apply the lessons in everyday scenarios around him/her.

We have made sure to include spaces for you to note your answers to lessons at the end of each section. It is our desire that you will take notes, but don't stop at that. We want you to apply the lessons by implementing the messages daily. But more importantly, learning without fun makes it a tedious venture. Therefore, we want you to have fun while learning.

This book is an insightful book filled with incredible ways which we can use to attain any height regardless of our fields. This book will build you as a leader, it will make you accountable and it will give you im mense growth. Shall we begin?

AUTHOR'S NOTE

Connectivity is at the Centre of what makes us human. It is safe to say that one of life's greatest and most precious gift is time. And for people to give theirs to one, one must treat with uttermost value and care.

Attention is important in connectivity. I believe that for one to connect to another person, they must be able to give their attention to you, however brief it is. This does not change the fact that sometimes nervousness can cause one to stumble and make mistakes. However, the single most important thing we must understand is, as humans, we must learn to connect with others. Regardless of our nervousness, regardless of how scared we are, we must learn to speak and to connect with others.

Speaking is vulnerability for it is not about quoting a bunch of memorized lines, givi ng stats or records, effective speaking is about connection and this is important for us as humans. Because we are not talking to robots or machines, but to people. People who have real emotions, fears and questions.

In talking to people, we may not be ab le to provide all the answers to every person, but we can do one thing every time, value the time being given to us by them. For this in itself is leading and leadership is a difficult endeavor. It takes courage, it takes commitment and attention to step i nto the arena of life, of dreams and passion, of career and work, it takes a daring courage to step in and lead the kind of life that one desires.

IT'S NOT THE CRITIC WHO COUNTS

Sometimes our greatest fears does not come from our inability or lack of experience of doing something, they come from what others might say about us. The President of United States in 1910, said these words, "It is not the critic who counts; not the man who points out how the strong man stumbles, or where the doer of deeds could have done them better," to remind us of how loud the voices of those who stay by the sidelines are. This President, Theodore Roosevelt, further tells us that "the credit belongs to the man in the arena..." this speech, 'Citizens in a Republic," has gone on to inspire many people in different cultures, it has shaped the lives of great men and women and been quoted a thousand times over. The inspiration drawn from this speech spoken in 1910 has giving many people the courag e to lead a life of courage, including the author.

Stumbled upon the quote in a time of great challenge, self-doubts and personal crisis, the author soon came to a conclusion that *the courage to be vulnerable is not about winning or losing, it's about the courage to show up when you can't predict or control the outcomes.*

Like many before her, the speech has inspired her greatly and challenged her to open herself up to the marvelous world continuous learning and creating. Part of such creation was, 'The Gift of Imperfection,' a book that introduced her research on the ten guideposts for wholeheartedness.

They are as follows:

1. Authenticity

2. Laughter, Song and Dance

3. Self-Compassion

4. Peaceful and Stillness

5. Resilient Spirit

6. Gratitude and Joy

7. Significant Labor

8. Intuition and Trusting Faith

9. Creativity

10. Play and Rest

Because *it's not the critic who counts, the* author has learnt to put herself out there, to dare to lead a life of courage. For it costs nothing to be nothing, to do nothing and to remain nothing. It takes courage to be something, it takes courage to live.

INTRODUCTION

"I have one deceptively and somewhat selfish goal for this book: I desperately want to share everything I've learnt with you..."

The author's opening statement is evidential of how much she wanted to share in the book **'Dare to Lead'**. She confessed her desire to share all that she knows, all she had learnt in her years of research, her experience working and interviewing captains of industries and more than a hundred CEOs on the future of leadership program evaluation. What is remarka ble is that she wanted the book to be one that can be read from cover to cover in a single flight and she made it so by writing in simple and clear terms.

Leadership is hard. Studying about it is simpler than actually leading. More than the research, inte rviews and studies, being a leader herself has taught her how hard and difficult it is to be a leader. To the writer, nothing is as difficult as leading, except maybe marriage and parenting. It is as though being in a class and learning the theoretical asp ect of a subject. It's usually fun, depending on who is teaching, how and where the teaching is taking place, but the application and practicality of what is taught is usually a different story entirely. Which is to say, learning, when it comes to leadersh ip is always easier. The difficult part is in the actual leading. And it goes without saying that it is the reason why many people find it hard to lead people.

The author admitted it in this book how hard it is to lead a person, especially when faced with major problems that requires critical thinking and problem solving. The courage and determination it takes to stay calm during immense pressure and the emotional pull required is what makes a leader a leader. Leadership, truly, is very difficult. It is th erefore no brainer why people, or supposed leaders, run away from the responsibilities of leadership. Because it is easier to bear the title of a 'leader,' than it is to lead people. People shy away from helping people grow by leading them from where they are and where they want to be often times because they themselves haven't learnt how to lead themselves. It is what our world has become, sad as it may be, there are only few leaders in the world.

For this reason, the author dreams of a world filled with leaders who wouldn't run away from responsibilities. A world with brave leaders, a world of daring and bold leaders who can discover the potential in people, who can be patient with people and not only understand their processes, but resist the urge of stepping in order to take the spot light. Leadership is being courageous, it is having the courage to be like the gardener who plants, nurtures and grows a flower, then watches it bloom beautifully. Leadership is developing people's potential and giving them the opportunity to be themselves.

The world needs leaders, leaders who will lead with all their hearts regardless of the sector they are called to serve. Leaders who will lead themselves and others in truth, honesty and openness, men and women who can se e beyond the now, beyond their own personal interests, but committed to building and developing people both for the short term and the long term. One important thing to note is that the author understands the human nature and how hard it is for someone to place the needs of others above their home. This book is therefore, a guide to learning how to lead the right way by understanding people's processes enough to not lead from a place of fear, hurt and assumption. And because such leaders are hard to find, w e do have a long way to go.

To shorten that journey or rather to discover and challenge leaders, is why this book was written, The author's aim is, more than anything, to challenge the perception of leadership and to try to change in it and pass on that safe world to her own children. And her intention is to make this book simpler and easier to read in one single flight.

Brave Leaders and Courage Cultures

Necessity they say is the mother of all inventions, how about curiosity? A curious mind is a mind in search and constantly seeking for new ways and answers to things. Having said that, we can state for a fact that the challenges and obstacles that daring leaders face are so real and intense. But what sets them apart from most ordinary people is the abil ity to keep searching for answers and new ways of creating a solution for every challenge or obstacle.

The author during her research discovered how vital it is for leaders to stay curious. In her research, she found out that what makes all the difference , irrespective of the situation, is the ability to stay curious and the courage to keep showing up. To have the courage to ask one's self logical and objective questions, to be curious about what could possibly be the solution to whatever challenge we face and the ability to show up regardless of how we feel or whether we have the answers or not, makes a world of difference. It cannot be overemphasized.

The potency of a problem, barrier or challenge weakens when we keep showing up. And nothing can stop us t hat way; for the way to move information from one's head to one's heart, is one's hands. Therefore, regardless of the sector or field, show up. Show up for your family. Show up for your business. Show up for you career. Show up for that dream or passion… don't stop showing up. Take those punches in the arena of life, swallow the difficulties and show up again. And again, show up. Keep showing up.

WHAT STANDS IN THE WAY BECOMES THE WAY

The book started with the author talking about her interviews with corporate global leaders on the need for a change in leadership style. It is no doubt that we currently live in a world that is so demanding and challenging, therefore, having leaders who can rise up to the occasion is of great necessity. The demand and the challenges we face today are enough to discourage us and make us shy away from responsibilities, which is why the author, as well as all the interviewees agreed that there is a rising need for brave new leaders and more courageous cultures.

Ask anyone what are the true qualities for brave leadership and you're most likely to hit a brick wall. The author, though faced a great challenge in trying to get clear and concise answers from the research participants on the specific skills that support brave leadership, was able to get these participants to identify behavioral patterns and cultural issues that can serve as barriers in the way of leadership in organizations across the globe:

1. Avoidance of tough conversations. This reminds me of the phrase, "a rumble in the deep," in order words, certain conversations exposes people's vulnerability and for this reason, they want to avoid them. This is why courage is needed. Due to lack of courage, peopl e also avoid conversations that require them to give honest feedbacks.

2. As leaders what we give our attention to matters a lot. It doesn't matter where or who we are leading, be it our family, or our small team of four in the business world, what we give our attention to can either serve as a building bridge to link us up with success and growth, or it can become a barrier that will limit us from moving forward. Supposed leaders often spend most of their time paying attention or addressing things that become a barrier eventually. As the author rightly noted, we spend most of our time addressing problematic behaviours, instead of giving our attention and time acknowledging and addressing the fears and feelings that comes with change or feelings that show up during change and challenges.

3. The shrinking line called 'trust'. People find it hard to lead because people cannot trust them and this is caused by their inability to show empathy or connect to others. Most times than not, they placed their needs and desires above that of others.

4. People are afraid of rejection. We live in a   world where people are afraid of critical scrutiny, so they would rather hide in the shadows and remain mediocre. Because the world is so fast paced and every day, some people are coming out with bold and innovative ideas, the majority find it hard to do. This is caused by a deep fear of rejection, therefore, people are not taking smart risks and

when we are afraid to create because we fear rejection or cannot take smart risks, one cannot expect us to put forth bold ideas.

5. A hold of the past. Letting go of hurt, failure or criticism can be one of the most difficult things to do as a leader. Often times we allow ourselves to be trapped in the past. Those setbacks, those disappointments and painful experiences lock us up within ourselves and it hampers growth and productivity. We spend most of our time trying to reassure members of our team who are questioning their contributions and value, instead of spending that amount of time creating and devising to make sure everything is made whole in the company. Everything, including ourselves.

6. There is little or no room for accountability because instead of addressing issues, we attack personality. We put blame and most times shame people, this is detrimental and can affect learning and growth.

7. Conversations on diversity and inclusivity is another major *arena* people are afraid of stepping into. Because it is such a sensitive issue, people are scared of being wrong or saying things that might be misunderstood. When we place our personal comfort over discussing certain issues, it will prevent us from having a discussion that can help us understand these issues better and seek for a way forward.

8. Every problem or challenge often present us with options of a quick fix or a grounded hard work to solve it. And the problem is we almost always opt for the quick and immediate fix. When faced with a difficult challenge, we should focus on first identifying and acknowledging that we have a problem, then we create a sustainable solution

to solve that problem. Otherwise, our *quick* pattern will cause the problem to resurface over and over again.

9. Measurability of values in organizations. Most organizations do not evaluate or assess the values of employees or individuals based on measurable behaviours but on immeasurable behaviours like aspirations. And when these values aren't measurable, we find it hard to evaluate or teach it.

10. Growth, I believe is intentional. I believe it is nobody's intention to fail in life or in leadership, regardless of the role. But fear has a way of limiting or stopping us from growing. And this fear, most times capitalizes on perfectionism. We find ourselves trapped and hampered by lack of productivity because we cannot recognize when it is *enough*. Fear and Perfectionism are two powerful weapons that can serve as a barrier to stop us from both personal and corporate growth.

The above list cut across all areas, both organizational and individual struggles. These problems and barriers will always arise, but as leaders, we should be able to identify the specific courage-building skill sets needed to tackle these problems.

For the reader to understand better, the author explains how she worked with her team, interviewing many more leaders and testing the developed instruments on the students in Jones Graduate School of Business at Rice University, the Kellogg School of Management at Northwestern University, and the Wharton School at the University of Pennsylvania. They were relentless in their search for an answer.

LET'S UNPACK WHAT WAS LEARNT.

The Heart of Daring Leadership

1 Every human wants to be comfortable and whatever threatens that comfort evokes a certain reaction. It can either be to confront the situation or to avoid it all together. Leadership is no different. People most times fear what they don't know. And not many know they can face the problem or challenges they are seemingly running away from. It takes courage to face and confront the challenges before us. This is one thing that distinguish daring leaders from the others.

Daring leaders have courage. They have the courage to face and handle difficult conversations, the courage to confront their fears and work on a mutually beneficial connectivity with others, at work, home or anywhere. However, this is not to say that daring leaders don't have fears. Or that they don't experience fear. No. on the contrary, they do. But the difference is, while experiencing fears, they build enough courage to face it, not run away from it. In man's nature of *take flight or fight* when confronted by challenges, daring leaders stay and fight. Courage and fear goes hand in hand and it is normal to experience both at the same time.

From this we can see that vulnerability is a major determinant to getting to courage. In order words, we must face or rumble with vulnerability before we get to courage.

Courage, the author says, is a collection of four skill sets that can be taught, observed and measured. They are as follows:

- ❖ Rumbling with Vulnerability
- ❖ Living into Our Values

❖ Braving Trust
❖ Learning to Rise

Though learning all these skills can be instrumental in our growth process and our ability to lead, the most important of them all is learning how to rumble with vulnerability. This is the foundation upon which all other skills should be built on. This will help you to put all the skills to effective use. All the skills are very important, but our capacity of becoming daring leaders , cannot be greater than our capacity for vulnerability.

In the author's research and experiments, this approach she said has been tested in over fifty organizations and with approximately ten thousand individuals, resulting in positive impact on how the leaders lead their respective teams and also the performance level of their teams. This she said is one of her reasons for writing this book; to help us with specific tools, practices and behaviors that can help us build our muscle memory for living these concepts.

2 In this book, the author helped us to understand a shocking, yet so subtle revelation on fear. Usually, we are taught to believe that fear is the single most powerful barrier than can stop us from achieving our goal or limitations on how we lead. But the author helps us to see it differently. *It is not fear that is the barrier, fear will always arise. How we respond to fear is the barrier.*

Another misconception that the author addressed, was the perception that courage is an inherent trait.   But this book helps us to understand that it is not about who we are as individuals that makes us lead daringly, it is how we behave and show up in difficult situations that makes all the difference. Why? Daring leadership isn't selfish. It doesn't seek to take the easier route by protecting ourselves when faced with situations that expose us to vulnerability. Rather, daring leaders summon courage to face it. The interviews pointed this out when they talked about how normal it is to feel many types of fear regularly, but what makes the difference is how we respond to these fears or feelings, especially the ones which brings us face to face.

The following chapters will teach you skills and examine the very things that get in our way of building courage. In t his process, you shall discover that self-awareness and self-love are important and yet powerful tools.

3 The spaces we create in today's worlds are all filled but yet empty, because they are void of empathy, respect or even connectivity. This is because we avoid tough conversation and avoid tough decisions. It has become a norm. And it is wrong. Because in the spaces we create, people don't feel safe, heard or respected in it.

The author didn't just tell us what kind of spaces we shouldn't build. Rather she showed us how we can build environments that thrive on bravery, innovation, problem solving and servic e to not just ourselves but to others. As leaders, if we can build environments like these, we will enjoy wholehearted relationships. This will allow people take off their armors, feel cared for and connected to. And if we can't or are not able to, it is okay to find someone else who can care and connect to them, in that way. There is no shame in doing that. Because sometimes, there are cases where despite how much commitment we make, we feel a certain disconnection with some people. Finding someone who is a better fit, shows we are daring leaders ourselves, this alone requires a lot of courage. Because understanding the commitment to care and connect is only the basics, it takes real courage to recognize when we can't fully serve the people we lead.

It doesn't matter where, in schools, places of worship, corporate settings, when we create spaces that give room for people to explore the world and rumble with vulnerability, we build wholehearted engagements that changes the trajectory of the lives of the people we lead and our own lives.

More than anything, the most important thing to know is that all these skills that makes up courage can be learned. They are also teachable and measurable. I think understanding this matters a lot. Because this will help us s top avoiding, it will help us jump into the arena and face our fears and feelings that get in the way of us becoming daring leaders.

INTRODUCTION ANALYSIS

The reader could see that the author was passionate about the subject matter. Her tone was that of excitement and desire to share everything with the leader. And by everything, I meant all she had learnt in her decades of research. A key lesson to learn is how she showed us that courage isn't an inherent trait. Nobody was born courageous. It is a set of skills, one that can be learned. The interview she conducted, her constant reference to them, helps us to understand that we are not alone in our struggle w ith perfectionism. And she did a fairly good job in exposing the futility of perfectionism. The introduction not only introduces us to what daring leadership is all about, the bravery and courage it takes to chart the course of their lives and that of othe rs, it shows us the most important thing of them all. The courage to step into the arena and rumble with vulnerability. For it is not enough to lead people by recognizing the potentials in them, understanding their process and building these potentials. We need to be able to lead ourselves first. Because only then can we be able to truly lead them not from a place of discomfort and fear, but from a place of courage and purpose. It is important to know that fear is inevitable in our day to day life, and situ ations will definitely arise to make us want to take flight. But our ability to stay and fight, by showing up and stepping into the arena shows that we are willing to become daring leaders.

PART ONE

CHAPTER ONE

THE MOMENTS AND THE MYTHS

When Roosevelt gave the Citizen in a Republic speech in 1910, I am sure he would never have known that it would be the saving grace to someone more than a hundred years later. Though, many, including athletes, authors, artistes, politicians and artists have been inspired by this quote, the light it shone on three key lessons for the author resonates more than most.

The first which she calls 'Physics of Vulnerability' simply means, if we are brave enough often enough, we will fall. For clarity sake, this means, no matter how strong we are, no matter how great our ability to dare is, we will definitely fall. It is a simple acknowledgement of the fact that everyone, including those we admire, goes through disappointments, hurts and failures. Yet, it doesn't mean that daring greatly means taking unwise risks. No. it's about acceptance of the inevitability of failure but yet willingness to give our all come what may.

The second lesson shows that vulnerability is that very emotion we experience in moments we're faced with uncertainty, risk and emotional exposure. This lesson explains what vulnerability is and it is not winning or losing, it is simply that courage to show up even when faced with uncertainty .

And the last of the lessons sharpened by Roosevelt's quote is, we should only take advice or get feedback from those who are in the arena having their ass kicked. In other words, if you're not willing to have the courage to face your own fears, I am not interested in anything you have to say.

Journeying up the route of vulnerability and courageous leadership, I think it's of great importance to make it clear that vulnerability isn't weakness. On the contrary, it is being brave. The author's research helps us to understand that the experiences that come with vulnerability aren't easy to handle. These experiences can make us anxious, fearful, and uncertain and cause us to be emotional unbalanced. This can cause us to put our guards up, or as she puts it, wear our armors of protection and choosing avoidance over vulnerability. It is really difficult to let ourselves be open and emotional exposed, it takes great courage to show up with a whole heart.

Speaking of showing up with a whole heart, it is important to know that the culture of avoidance is something that takes courage to break. In fact many would encourage this potent yet weak culture that drives further the rifts and spaces between us and severs connectivity. But the third lesson the author mentioned should tell us a lot about who we take advice from. In other words, don't take advice from people who aren't daring to live, love or face that difficult conversation or situation, but can easily point faults in what we are doing, judge our actions, pick holes in our ideas and innovations, criticize and question our motives, and even throw darts of advice on what and how they think it should be. These kinds of people are dangerous to our growth. These people come with cheap -seats feedbacks and they spread fear, uncertainty, cynicism and criticism to discourage us from daring greatly. These people make us wear armors and hamper our connectivity.

However, it is inevitable that hurtful comments, feedbacks and unsolicited advice from these kinds of people will surely come. When they do, we sometimes try to figure a way to give a ground breaking comeback. This is wrong and harmful to us. Because in the process of doing that, of nursing the thoughts of a great comeback, we can end up growing hates in our hearts. The sad thing is that sometimes those hurtful comments inspired by those outside the arena confirm our deepest and worst fears. But no matter what, we must leave it all on the ground, less it grows a seed in us.

We must also understand that feedback is necessary for our growth. Good or bad, they can be instrumental in helping us chart the course of our lives. Therefore, we must not shield ourselves from feedbacks. We must be open to them. Because they help us evaluate and reevaluate our stand or viewpoint. But despite that, we shouldn't be open to *all* feedbacks. No. We mustn't engage with all feedbacks, because when we do, irrespective of the qua lity of the feedback or the intention behind it, if it hurts too much, it can cause us to armor up and as a result, disconnect us from vulnerability.

Sometimes, self-protection stops us from being hurt, but at the same time hampers our growth. Never shou ld we trade it over love. Though many equate it as weakness, but love isn't weakness. To love is to be vulnerable and most times, those who we love have the tendency to hurt us.

For the sake of clarity, we can know which opinion matters to us by learning from the author's book. In it, she explained we can simply write down the names of the people whose opinion matters to us. What we should do then is to take time, at least, ten minutes to reach out to them and share a little gratitude.

These people must be people who care enough to be honest and real with you, people who are not afraid to tell you the truth, but kind enough to help you through it.

The following are guideposts on how to choose these people:

- They should be people who love you wholeheartedly , not despite your vulnerability and imperfections, but because of them. They should not be a "yes" people.

- They should be people who can look you squarely in the eye and rumble with your vulnerability. People who wouldn't shy away from telling you when you are in the wrong even when it is with a subordinate and you need to apologize. Yet, they will be there to support you through dealing with the feeling that comes with it.

These kinds of people are people who would make you come face to face with your fears and lovingly force you to face your vulnerability after a major setback, but they would be there to nurture you back to life and peace.

THE FOUR SIX MYTHS OF VULNERABILITY

In the author's other book 'Daring Greatly,' she explained four 'Myths of Vulnerability' which are misguided myths. But in this book, she explained that rather than four, there are six misguided myths. And they are as follows:

Myth #1: Vulnerability is weakness.

A lot of people, including leaders of organizations, believe that vulnerability is a weakness. And because they are used to project that sense of purpose and that aura of power, they can't afford to be vulnerable or portray anything that will make them appear weak. They want to always show they are brave and courageous, which is not a bad thing. But they are wrong because they are doing the opposite of what they think they are portraying. One cannot truly experience courage without experi encing vulnerability. Vulnerability in itself is being courageous.

Myth #2: I don't do vulnerability.

This myth is strong because it's a myth of denial. When people say they don't deal with vulnerability, they are either in denial or they don't understand what it is. It's not a thing of choice, to accept or not to accept vulnerability. One cannot do without it. It's either you face it or it faces you. Dealing with it teaches one to step into the arena of vulnerability, rumble with it, understand how it can affect and drive our behaviors, so we will not find ourselves acting outside of our values and integrity. On the other hand, not dealing with vulnerability is only exposing ourselves to fear. And whether we like it or not, whether we admit it or not, fear always has a way of driving our thinking and our behavior.

The author encourages us to talk to those within our squad, ask them how we act when we feel vulnerable. This will help us to know exactly where we are operating from when dealing with vulnerability. Whether it's from a place of self-awareness or a place of terminal uniqueness, feedbacks from our square squad will help us understand how we act in times when we are vulnerable.

Myth #3: I can do it alone.

We can never walk alone as long as we l ive and walk on this earth. We are social species. We are built for connectivity, for network and for community. Therefore, no matter what we may think, we need people. It is expected that some people who have faced hurt in the past might want to disagree,   but it is the truth. We need people. In the absence of people, in the absence of real and authentic connection, we begin to suffer. We suffer because that's the way we are hardwired. This is not to say that we should need people for self-validation, or ac ceptance or changing who we are just to be acceptable to them. It is in being self -aware, as well as being open to receiving honest feedback from those in our square squad.

Myth #4: You can engineer the uncertainty and discomfort out of vulnerability.

Over the past years, we have seen the magic of technology. We have seen what a true miracle it is. It has made our lives simpler and brought about ease in our daily living. But despite all these wonderful things that technology has done for us, it still lac ks something very important. It lacks human connectivity that fosters connectional experience. In other words, it doesn't matter how much advancement we make on technology (e.g. AI) it cannot fix our vulnerability or the human experience that comes with relationship. However, our avoidance culture is pushing us to developing an app that helps with vulnerability, apps that tells us when to have the hard conversation for a healthier connection. But no, there are no short cuts or quick fix. No app created can completely take away relational vulnerability. We must face vulnerability in the arena and rumble with it.

Myth #5: Trust comes before vulnerability.

When one has been hurt in the past, it's usually very difficult to open oneself to trust again. Which is why to trust is to be courageous. We cannot say for certain that trust comes before vulnerability or vulnerability before trust. But what we can agree on is the fact that we need to trust for us to be vulnerable and in the same vain, we need to be vulnerable to be able to build trust. However, the popular notion of what trust is can be limiting and damaging if care isn't taken. Trusting is not an action, trusting is a process; a process made whole by series of corresponding actions. And it takes time and courage to build. Also, a disturbing misconception of how trust is earned has been widely reinforced through popular culture. It is believed that there m ust be a heroic deed, or saintly or magnificent visible action. No. Trust is earned in small moments.

Myth #6: Vulnerability is disclosure.

Building a team takes a whole lot than just gathering people together. Sharing moments and activities that foster s connectivity and vulnerability is essential to building an effective team. However, leaders are often weighed down by the challenges of how much or how little to share with their teams. To address this, the author points out the fact that vulnerability is not just in the multitudes of information shared, the medium through which it is shared but also it matters where it is shared. Which is to say, a leaders primary job is to create a safe space for members of the team to take risk and be vulnerable at the same time in front of others? This is in itself is psychological safety, this is what sets successful teams apart.

However, it is important to know that you shouldn't over share (sharing without boundaries, is not vulnerability, it is confession), do not share and leave scanty information that makes it hard to connect with you. While sharing, let these thoughts guide, "why am I sharing, with whom I am sharing and what are our different roles." Then honestly ask yourself if it is productive.

TO FEEL IS TO BE VULNERABLE

We all crave to be heard, to be seen and to be understood. As social creatures, it is important to know that we are hardwired to want to know what people—especially the ones we love and trust—think or feel about us. It is only natural.

But, sometimes, some feedbacks can hit so deeply it can cause us to fight or take flight, especially when they come from those who are our subordinates or the ones we lead, be it in our families, workplace or places of worship. I can say authoritatively that this is the reason why we sometimes avoid conversations. We do this because we want to protect ourselves.

Talking about feedbacks from our subordinates, of a truth, it also takes daring courage for those who we lead to step into the arena of that difficult conversation. It is a great deal to look at your leader and give them an open, honest and frank feedback, especially unpleasant ones. This is because they stand the chance of being perceived as an enemy. But when looked at critically, we would find out that they are not truly the enemy. The fact that their feedback rumbled with our vulnerability doesn't mean that they are the enemy. What this means is that, it will require courage on our own part to face the situation by having that difficult conversatio n without perceiving them as enemies.

Another practice which is common among the leaders who lack courage is the habit of avoidance because they are trying to be nice. No. We should never avoid conversation because we are trying to be nice to the other pe rson. That is wrong. Contrary to our perception of this being kind, it is actually us being unkind and unfair. Why?

Because, when we avoid telling people what they need to know that can help them one way or the other, and we feed those half-truths or bull shit, we are being unkind and unfair to them. And I hate to tell us that it is also selfish. This is because, in all truths, we are not doing it for them, we are doing it for us because we lack courage.

Another thing the author pointed out is the need to not shield ourselves from feedback. For growth to truly take place in our lives, be it in family, spiritual or organizational growth, we mustn't shield ourselves from feedback. This is because some feedbacks will help us evaluate and reevaluate our stand o r viewpoint on many different things. But even at that, we mustn't engage with all feedback. Because, when we do, irrespective of the quality of the feedback or the intention behind it, if it hurts too much, it can cause us to armor up and as a result disc onnect us from vulnerability.

Lastly, we should never get to a place where we trade self - protection over love. Though there are great chances that we will do this, we should not. Why? Because to love is to be vulnerable.

But this poses a question.... how do we know which opinion matters to us?

The author answered this same question in her other book, 'Daring Greatly'.

Try it here.

Take a piece of paper, write down the names of people whose opinions of you matter. This people are your square -squad. Take ten minutes to reach out to them, and share a little gratitude. Here is a sample from the author:

"I'm getting clear on whose opinions matter to me. Thank you for being one of those people. I'm grateful that you care enough to be honest and real with me."

CHAPTER ANALYSIS

This section is packed with deep truths. And also, set the pace for the entire book. One thing that made this chapter great is that the author demystified a lot of myths about vulnerability. There are lots of things to learn from this chapter.

Lesson

1. To be vulnerable is not the same thing as to be weak.

2. What it means to be daring is to take decision or act on something even in times when we are not sure.

3. To be careful who we take advice from. We should only take advice from people who are themselves daring and in the arena like us.

4. For growth to take place we must listen to feedbacks, but not all feedbacks are necessary.

Issues surrounding the subject matter

1. Why do people perceive vulnerability as a weakness?

_____

2. How do we face or go into a difficult conversation especially with someone or people whom we have a terrible past with?

_____

3. Do you agree that feedbacks are necessary for growth even the ones from your square squad?

_____

3. What are the myths surrounding vulnerability and how do we demystify them?

_____

Goals

1. How can you learn from rumbling with vulnerability?

_____

2. In what way can you rise up to become a daring leader if you let go of self-protection?

_____

3. The complexity and the frailty/sensitive of vulnerability makes leaders want to avoid it. How can you engage in it, to improve on relationship?

_____

5. Can you take feedback, however harsh, and not want to give a perfect reply or comeback?

_____

   1. How can you share wholeheartedly and still respect the other person's boundaries and yours too?

_____

Actions

We must be open and willing to rumble with vulnerability, by being open to feedback but not all feedbacks.

Checklist

There is no way to avoid feedbacks, and feedbacks can cause us to want to act first without factoring how such can be a process of learning for us. So, we should learn to take feedback, rumble with vulnerability and grow.

CHAPTER TWO

CLEAR IS KIND. UNCLEAR IS UNKIND

THE CALL TO COURAGE

When we talk about courage we are talking about vulnerability, because one cannot exist without the other. Often times, courage is portrayed as being independently whole and without fear. But that isn't true. Courage is knowing fully that there is fear but looking past it. Courage is kindness to self and to others; to look past that uncomfortable feeling of fear and be clear on the subject matter. Courage is not choosing our own comfort over the truth. So, regardless of how we feel or how it makes the other person feel, having the courage to voice our truth says a lot about our person.

This is because, when having a difficult conversation, we often want to bolt out of the conversation by saying, okay, I get it. Most times we feel it is safer to just run the other way and avoid such conversations because they are uncomfortable. But we need to learn how to stick with it. Don't run from such conversations. Stay and face that difficult conversation. However, sometimes when we muster enough courage to have that difficult conversation we often make the mistake of pushing through it. This can be damaging. It is okay to ask for a break or take a break from the conversation and reconvene later.

Also, it is important to not e, when having such conversation we might be lured by our emotions of *I am not enough* or *I am better than them all;* the both of which are wrong. This is because we are often exposed in the arena and the persistent blows of emotions could force us to enter th e ring of comparisons; telling ourselves, we are better than the others and why should we have to listen to them when they are nowhere better than us. Avoid such.

Treasure hunt

It is important that we understand the value of something sometimes so we wouldn't abuse it. Let us ask ourselves what treasure it is we seek before we start searching for it in the first place. We'll be on a futile journey if we do not understand what it is we are searching, therefore this question is of utmost importance.

Ask yourself this question, it would help you be clear on your objectives and to make clear and concise decisions. When you do this, it would help you take your fears into consideration, improve your expectations and make it more realistic and also help you to understand your process.

THE POWER AND WISDOM TO SERVE OTHERS

Service is key to changing the world, selfless service is key to changing the people who can join us in our quest to change the world for the better. Ho wever, it is true what they say, if you want to change the world, start with the man in the mirror. Most times we are often consumed by what is wrong with the world that we might fail to see what is wrong in us ourselves. But until we can learn to be comfo rtable confront our own weaknesses and be vulnerable, we can't truly serve others. How do we get others to be vulnerable if we will not be vulnerable ourselves?

To be candid, people are used to the comfort that comes with avoiding uncomfortable things. This might not be their intention, but as a result of a culture borne out of habit. Even people who candidly want to be vulnerable, people who want to talk about the hard stuffs and hold up spaces that encourages others to safely talk about what they face , can't talk because they don't know how to. Sometimes, the problem is no other than the language barrier. It is important we know that in this case , it is not about trying to change tongues or speak in other dialects, but the knowledge and wisdom of picking the right words, knowing when to use them and where to use them. This is because sometimes, where you say something to someone has as much power as what and how you say that thing to that person. This it is true service.

Life is all about service. And to serve better, we must first learn how to face our fears. We must find courage to enter the dark cave of our lives and face ourselves, like Lucas Skywalker. Just like the author pointed out about her loving Joseph Campbell's advice to Lucas Skywalker in the movie, Star Wars. *"When you find the courage to enter that cave, you're never going in to secure your own treasure or your own wealth; you face your fears to find the power and wisdom to serve others."*

It is also important to understand that service to others doesn't mean denying yourself or being unkind to your own self. Service to others means being true and honest with yourself first, facing your fears and holding up spaces to help others face theirs too. Also, when people come to you or people who you know are going through tough times, it is important to know what to say to them. Though finding the right things to say to them matters a lot, but more than spea king, listen. Listen when they start talking. Don't talk, or wait to talk with a formulated response. Just listen.

Also, when having conversations like this we are often tempted to want to take responsibility for their emotions. Create spaces between you and them when having conversations like this. You can acknowledge their emotions, but don't own them. Let them bare their hearts out, but set boundaries. Set boundaries that they shouldn't cross. However, be observant of yourself so you won't sink under the weight of the emotions they are pouring out. When it is getting difficult for you too or for them, you can take a break and reconvene. What this does is to give them enough room to thoroughly think and also to circle back. In a nutshell, it is courageous to acknowledge people's feelings; in fact it takes a lot of courage. But to take responsibility for those feelings is unwise and dangerous for both you and for the person.

CHAPTER ANALYSIS

The author started by talking about her team. She talked about how she had to be vulnerable in the rumbling process with her team and the lessons learnt are enormous. One interesting thing that stood out was how she painted those emotions that often drive our thinking and behaviour when faced with uncertainty or receiving harsh feedback.

Lesson

1. Be clear and concise when giving feedback to someone.

2. Avoiding conversations, especially difficult conversation, is cowardly. It shows we are trying to protect ourselves, not the people we should be having that conversation with.

3. Being courageous means facing your fears.

4. Talk to people rather than talk about them.

5. Don't push through hard conversations. Sometimes it is okay to take a break and come back to that subject lat er after you might have thought about it clearly.

Issues Surrounding the Subject Matter.

1. Why do people avoid difficult conversations?

_____

2. What does it mean to serve others?

_____

—

3. How do we face our fears?

_____

—

4. How do we create safe spaces for people to talk?

_____

—

Goals

1. How can you be more courageous?

_____

2. Who are the people you need to summon courage to have some difficult conversation

_____

3. What are the things you need to do to be clear and kind?

_____

4. What are the things you need to do to be safe aware?

_____

5. How can you prevent your ego from setting in when receiving   feedbacks?

_____

6. How can you create spaces in your workplace that encourages   openness   and   rumbling?

_____

7. How do you constantly show up and not get exhausted?

_____

Actions

1. Try to not to see people giving feedback as the enemy, but be sure who your square squad are; so you can go into difficult conversation, knowing you it will be a learning experience.

2. We should expose ourselves in the arena of that difficult conversation and build more courage.

Checklist

1. Courage isn't built in a day. It takes constant practice.

CHAPTER THREE

THE AMORY

What is the symbol of love?

What is the gateway to emotional human experience?

The human heart...

There is no argument on the importance of the human heart in a man's body. It is the single most valuable part of a man's body. Like a valuable treasure it is carefully secured between the lungs, between the cubicles of the chest. Like a guarded safe, it is well protected due to its importance. It is not just because it's that one organ in our body that pumps and circulate blood in our body; it is because it is also that part of our body that answers the above question... it is the gateway to emotional experience and also it is the very symbol of love.

Whether we know it or not, each time we armour up to self-protect, we are sinking our hearts. We create layers upon layers trying to self-protect instead of practicing wholeheartedness. And what is wholeheartedness?

Wholeheartedness is our ability to accept our imperfection and celebrate our uniqueness. That is it. And to practice this is to be courageous. We can do this by learning how to integrate and put ourselves out there, be it in our homes, places of worship or places of work; especially places of work. It is hard to do that in our workplaces most times. This is because most organizations preach what they don't have nor create the environment to practice. This can be very frustrating and discouraging at the same time.

Whenever I hear things like bring your whole self to work, my question is usually; how does that environment treat the whole of me? How can it deal with my vulnerability? What if I do and I get hurt along the line? And I am sure a whole lot of us ask ourselves these questions too.

When you look at it critically you'd see that this is among the many things that cause people to armour up in marriages, in places of worship and at their places of work. Some organizations, however, in a bid to make productivity and management easier, severs emotions completely. This is so dangerous and it is like locking the heart up in a cold dark chamber.

Organizations should learn how not to do that. Because humans are emotional beings and the heart is the centre of emotions. It doesn't matter if they show it or not, they are emotional beings. On one hand we depend on our physical heart to pump and circulate blood to every part of our body, on the other hand we depend on our emotional heart to keep vulnerability alive in our veins.

It is also imperative that we do not give room for ego, otherwise we would find ourselves dealing with terminal uniqueness. The ego is that tiny part of us that craves acceptance, pleasing, performing, pretending... It's loud and protective. Think of the ego as a loud mouth drawing attention to himself, performing for all to see, pretend and protecting us to our own detriment. The ego is a con artist

standing in the arena of our life hustling us and shutting down the spark of our lives. The cynicism

ARMOURED LEADERSHIP VS DARING LEADERSHIP

DRIVING PERFECTIONISM AND FOSTERING FEAR OF FAILURE	MODELLING AND ENCOURAGING HEALTHY STRIVING, EMPATHY AND SELF-COMPASSION
WORKING FROM SCARCITY AND SQUANDERING OPPORTUNITIES FOR JOY AND RECOGNITION	PRACTICING GRATITUDE AND CELEBRATING MILESTONES AND VICTORIES
NUMBING	SETTING BOUNDARIES AND FINDING REAL COMFORT
PROPAGATING THE FALSE DICHOTOMY OF VICTIM, VIKING, CRUSH OR BE CRUSHED	PRACTICING INTEGRATION-STRONG BACK, SOFT FRONT, WILD HEART
BEING A KNOWER AND BEING RIGHT	BEING A LEANER AND GETTING IT RIGHT

HIDING UNDER CYNICISM	MODELING CARITY, HONESTY AND HOPE
USING CYNICISM & SELF-PROTECTION	MAKING CONTRIBUTIONS AND TAKING RISKS
USING POWER OVER	USING POWER WITH, POWER TO AND POWER WITHIN
HUSTLING FOR OUR WORTH	KNOWING OUR VALUE
LEADING FOR COMPLIANCE AND CONTROL	CULTIVATING COMMITMENT AND SHARED PURPOSE
WEAPONIZING FEAR AND UNCERTAINTY	ACKNOWLEDGING, NAMING AND NORMALIZING COLLECTIVE FEAR AND UNCERTAINTY
REWARDING EXHAUSTION AS A STATUS SYMBOL AND	MODELING AND SUPPORTING REST, PLAY AND RECOVERY

ATTACHING PRODUCTIVITY TO SELF-WORTH	
TOLERATING DISCRIMANTION, ECHO CHAMBERS AND A "FITTING IN" CULTURE	CULTIVATING A CULTURE OF BELONGING, INCLUSIVITY AND DIVERSE PERSPECTIVES
COLLECTING GOLD STAR	GIVING GOLD STARS
ZIGZAGGING AND AVOIDING	STRAIGHT TALKING AND TAKING ACTIONS
LEADING FROM HURT	LEADING FROM HEART

CHAPTER ANALYSIS

The human heart inarguably is the most important part of a man's body. The author explained to us that the importance of the human heart is beyond the pumping and circulation of blood. She showed us that it is important because it is the gateway to human experience by linking it to a valuable piece of treasure, one which is often guarded safely. But it is to our own disadvantage that we build up walls trying to self -protect.

Lesson

1. The human heart is the very centre of the human experience and the gateway to our emotional experience.

2. To protect it, we find ourselves armouring up.

3. Wholeheartedness is an acceptance of our weakness and celebration of our uniqueness.

4. We should never give ears to our egos, it is to our own peril.

Issues Surrounding the Subject Matter.

1. Why do people armour up so much, especially at the workplace?

_____

2. How can organizations create safe spaces for people to   loosen   up?

_____

—

3. How do we completely ignore our egos in moments when we feel the need to please, perform or pretend for acceptance?

_____

—

Goals

1. How can you be more wholehearted?

_____

2. Which would you rather pick, armored leadership or daring leadership?

Actions

1. Try to silence ego and not armor up.

Checklist

1. Be a daring leader, by being wholehearted and vulnerable when you must in order to foster good working relationship, trustworthiness and open a channel of communication.

CHAPTER FOUR

SHAME AND EMPATHY

The truth is like a bitter pill, it is hard to swallow. What makes it really hard to swallow most times is our ego. Ego does nothing positive in our lives. Absolutely nothing. It simply validates and heightens existing problems. Ego always appears though protecting us, but in the real sense it is harming us. What it does is to shield us from shame each time we face uncertainty or receive feedbacks that shakes us deeply. Why this is dangerous is because, shielding us from shame, is like trying to shut down our emotions completely. And this is bad.

Another thing it does is to protect us by activating that feeling of terminal uniqueness. It tells us we are better than everyone else and this is very risky. No matter how difficult it is, we must learn to rumble with vulnerabi lity by dealing with shame, not shutting ourselves to it or letting it overwhelm us.

The following are things you should know about shame:

1. Shame is universal
2. The word 'Shame' is uncomfortable to even talk about, so we are afraid to talk a bout it.
3. The less we talk about shame the more control it has over us.

What is Shame?

Before I define shame, I would like to reiterate the fact that we are social animals and we cannot do without connections to people, our environment and to ourselves. Having said that, Shame is that feeling of what we have done or failed to do that disconnects or makes us unworthy to be here. Because connection, love and belonging are the reasons we are here on this planet.

How to recognize Shame

It is quite easy to recognize Shame. It only speak s with two different voices. One says, "You're not good enough," the other says, "Who do you think you are?"

SHAME, GUILT, EMBARRASSMENT, HUMILIATION

For the purpose of clarity, I would like to clearly differentiate shame, guilt, embarrassment and humiliation. This is because they look alike and are often mistaken for the other. Guilt is that feeling that, I have done something wrong/bad. But shame is t hat feeling that tells us we are not able to do that thing because we are not enough.

Contrary to the behaviours or the unhealthy practice s of many, shame is not a compass for moral behaviours. It is almost guaranteed, where shame exists there is almost a lways no empathy. The opposite of experiencing shame is empathy. I am sure you've heard people say he/she is so shameless. In most cases, those people are empathy less , not shameless.

Humiliation on the other hand is that feeling that comes with us been criticised for what we did that might or might not be wrong. For embarrassment, it is almost the same. However, when we do something embarrassing, we don't feel alone. We know other people have done the same thing, and somehow we know that the way we feel doesn't define us and the feeling shall pass.

HOW SHAME SHOWS UP IN ORGANIZATIONS

Here are the things to watch out for in organizations to be able to recognize how Shame shows:

- Perfectionism
- Favouritism
- Gossiping
- Back-channelling
- Comparison
- Self-worth tied to productivity
- Harassment
- Discrimination
- Power over
- Bullying
- Blaming
- Teasing
- Cover-ups

SHAME RESILIENCE

Shame Resilience is defined by the author as, "the ability to practice authenticity when we experience shame, to move through the experience without sacrificing our values, and to come out on the other side of the shame experience with more courage, compassion, and connection than we had going into it."

To go through shame is inevitable. As long as we are in this life, we are going to experience shame . We can't avoid going through it at one point in our life. But we can feel better, knowing shame resilience is a learnable and teachable skill that can help us stay true to our core values all through the tumbling times of rumbling with our vulnerability.

Resilience is simply, moving from shame to empathy. And, oh yes, empathy is the real antidote to shame. S hame, the author said, is a social concept—it happens between people and it heals between people. So, since it happens and heals between people, we must share our shame with people who are understanding and loving.

EMPATHY

Before I explain empathy as de fined by the author, it is important to state that empathy is not sympathy. Matter of fact, the author explained that empathy is greatly misunderstood. Empathy is almost, always confused for sympathy. This is because to empathize is confused for playing the role of an adviser or someone who gives judgment in the guise of concern.

In the book, the author shared a very touching story of her daughter's final field hockey game. It happened that she was going to be away but had planned to show up as a surprise. On that day she had to fly down from another state with a friend, Suzanne and she was so excited that things were going to go as planned. But soon as she realized she wasn't going to make it to the game due to flight issues, she began to cry. Knowing how hard she had prepared for the game and how she wanted to show up for daughter, her friend, Suzanne was not just there with her, she was there for her. And despite this, she showed her no sympathy nor did she try to fill up the spaces with *I want you to feel better words.* As a friend she was there. When she needed to hear the hard truth, she dished it out to her, gently but honestly. She also wouldn't allow her to have comparative suffering. The situation was bad and there was nothing she could do.

This story for me, explains these words, "Empathy is not connecting to an experience, and it is connecting to the emotions that underpin an experience."

When we connect to others through sympathy it is always a weak connection. But empathy is deep and it is strong. And despite this, it is choosing to be vulnerable. Empathy is choosing to connect with another person by connecting with something in ourselves that truly knows the feeling that the other person is experiencing. Naturally, as humans, when having a difficult conversation with people, we often want to make them feel better when we see them in pains. We are in a hurry to give advice because we want to fix things. We are humans, it is our nature. However, let's not mistake that for empathizing. On the contrary, Empathy is that tough decision to not try to fix. In the author's words, "It is the brave choice to be with someone in their darkness—not to race to turn on the light so we feel better."

Empathy Skill #1: To see the world as others sees it, or perspective taking.

Our view of the world varies in a terribly wide margin. The lens through which I perceive the world is different from the lens through which you perceive the world. We see the world differently and that's okay. The lens through which we view the world is as a result of our history and our experience. But the mistake we usually make is to believe that we can take off our lenses, and try to view the world through someone else's lens. We can't. This is because our lenses are uniquely ours. However, despite how our lens differs from others, we can honour their unique perspectives as truth as much as we believe ours is the truth. The only difference is our perspective.

Empathy Skill #2: To be Non-judgmental

According to the author's research, there are two ways to ascertain when we are going to judge others:

1. We judge in areas where we feel we're most susceptible to shame

2. And we judge the people who are doing worse than we are in those areas.

Look out for these and you will not judge others.

Empathy Skill #3: To understand another person's feelings

Empathy Skill #4: To communicate your understanding of that person's feelings

In the book, both skills were combined due to how connected they are. To communicate our understanding of someone's emotion, we must first connect to our own feelings. In other words, to fluently speak the language of feelings, we must be in touch with our very own feelings.

This is what the author calls emotional literacy. Being fluent in the language of feelings, is to understand emotional literacy. However, some emotions are difficult to understand or process. Examples of two emotions which are very difficult to process are Shame and Grief. People find it hard to communicate these two emotions, and sometimes the only way they know how is to communicate them through anger or silence. While this is bad on its own, we live in a culture which practices the acceptan ce of being angry over being hurt. The society makes it look okay when you express how angry you are, but frowns at you expressing how hurt you are. Why? Because people aren't comfortable with that. If you can understand this, you will learn to look beyond how society has conditioned you to feel or express how you feel, dig deep and ask yourself what is l aying at the bottom of that feeling.

Empathy Skill #5: Mindfulness

According to Kristin Neff, Mindfulness is "taking a balanced approach to negative emotions so that feelings are neither suppressed nor exaggerated."

Therefore, we cannot completely ignore our pain and feel compassion for it at the same time.

WHAT EMPATHY LOOKS LIKE

Honestly, we must admit that we are all different and this difference in itself is not bad. We are from different backgrounds, we have different experiences and history. Therefore, what empathy looks like to you might not be what it looks like to me. All we need to do is just pay attention and then connect. Often times whe n having a difficult conversation, especially with people going through tough times, we let the fear of saying the wrong things stop us from actually saying anything. We shouldn't. And sometimes, it might not be fear of saying the wrong thing that stops us , it might be because we are driven by the desire to fix things or give the perfect response to heal that person's wounds. What we say does matter, how and where we say it too, but sometimes it is okay to connect with people with more than mere words. In other words, you don't need to have the perfect answer or response, just pay close attention and connect.

EMPATHY IN PRACTICE

There is a popular saying that came to mind while reading what the author said about this section, "We can't give what we don't have." It is the truth. You can't truly help someone from a broken place. I'm not saying you must be perfectly whole, there's no such thing. All I am saying is, you must at least be in a safe place in order to help others find safety. Empathy practice is simply finding those who have earned the right to hear our story, people who embrace us for our strengths and struggles and then connect with them. Doing this would help us be the right kind of connection for others in need and struggling for connections.

Though finding these kinds of people or just that one person can be a futile effort sometimes, but it works. It only takes practice. And also, does being that right person. When it comes to empathy, it's a matter of the right person, at the right time, on the right issues.

The following are the six known barriers

Empathy Miss #1: Sympathy vs. Empathy

Empathy is feeling with people. Sympathy is feeling for them. Empathy fuels connection. Sympathy drives disconnection.

Empathy Miss #2: The Gasp and Awe

This is another huge miss. When you tell someone or they hear your story and immediately start feeling shame on your behalf — then you have to be the one to make them feel better.

Empathy Miss #3: The Mighty Fall

The perfectioni sm lens. When someone thinks or perceives you as one who can't err, a pillar of perfection, they will never be able to help you when you talk to them. This is because they are viewing you through the lens of perfectionism.

Empathy Miss #4: The Block and Tackle

This is when you're scolded for what you did by your friend or the person you talk to because they are uncomfortable in dealing with vulnerability. You will hear things like: "How did you let this happen?

What were you thinking?"

Empathy Miss #5: The Boots and Shovel

These ones are the ones with the fluffy talk to make you feel better because they can't or don't want to connect to the emotions you're feeling. They tell you it is not that bad, or tell you how awesome or amazing you are, just so they can get away with not connecting with it themselves . As the author puts it, they are hustling to make you feel better, not hearing anything you feel, and not connecting to any emotion that you're describing.

Empathy Miss #6: If You Think That's bad…

Some if not most of us have friends like this. The ones who when we tell what happened to us or share our shame with, they immediately jump into a story of what happened to them before the Newton discovered the Law of Motion or before Olaus Roemer discovered the Speed of Light. They are the kind of friends, who systematically takes the focus off you and refocus it on themselves.

HOW TO PRACTICE SELF-COMPASSION

It is really a sad thing that people who intend to help others by showing them compassion are themselves void of self-compassion. We are often too gentle with others and too hard on ourselves. It is dangerous and can affect us in so many ways. We are hard on ourselves and often find it hard to forgive ourselves, especially when we feel we have messed up. We must learn how to show kindness to ourselves. We must learn to forgive our mistakes, let go of our pasts, and be gentle and understanding of our process.

As the author rightly put it, *"Talk to yourself the way you'd talk to someone you love. Most of us shame, belittle, and criticize ourselves in ways we'd never think of doing to others."*

EMPATHY AND SHAME RESILIENCE

There are four elements of shame resilience. And they are as follows:

1. Recognizing Shame and Understanding Its Triggers

Whenever shame washes over us, our first reaction is to try to shut it down. Don't. When shame starts to wash over us, we should learn how to feel our way through it and also try to understand what triggered it.

2. Practicing Critical Awareness

Shame can make us feel as though we are all alone in this world. It can make us feel so helpless because what it does is to show us our struggles and flaws through a magnified lens. At one point or the other in our lives, we will feel this way. It's inevitable. During times like this, we will feel as though something is wrong with us, or we are all alone in this big world. However, if we can learn how to zoom out of that feeling, we will see that we are not alone and there are others going through exactly what we are going through, if not worse.

3. Reaching Out

We also should practice reaching out to people. Because, most of the experiences that isolate us and make us feel as though we are all on our own in this world are often universal. By this I mean, we are not the only ones facing them. When we can learn how to reach out to people, we will find out that we are not alone in our struggles and shame.

3. Speaking shame

Another thing that Shame is good at is crippling our tongues. Haven't you noticed that most times you find the answers to things faster when you speak up? But when we keep silent, we tend to prolong our own suffering. This is what Shame thrives on. Silence. In silence it can amplify our pain and thrive in it. The best way to combat this is by speaking up. When yo u speak up, Shame loses its power and then you can ultimately destroy it.

Lastly, it is important to know that empathy is at the very centre of connection with self and with others; it is a reminder that we are not alone, and it isn't genetically hardwired to our makeup. It is learnable, as well as teachable. And we should, because as the poet June Jordan wrote, "We are the ones we have been waiting for."

CHAPTER ANALYSIS

There are so many information and lessons on this section, yet the author tried so much in making it very understandable. The section captures the true meaning of empathy and gives us a detailed explanation on what Shame is. The author's explanation helps us to understand our connectivity with others and an insight on what to do in having these difficult conversations.

Lesson

1. Ego acts like a friend but it is the enemy.

2. We should never shut down Shame so we can feel better, we must rumble with it.

3. Shame is Universal, everybody feels it.

4. Empathy is the opposite of Shame.

5. We empower shame when we stay silent.

6. Shame, guilt, humiliation and embarrassment are all different, and we must understand them to be able to handle them.

Issues Surrounding the Subject Matter.

1. How do we recognize the voice of shame?

_____

2. What other way does shame show up in organizations?

_____

–

3. If empathy isn't the same as sympathy, why does it appear like it most of the time?

_____

–

Goals

1. How can you learn the skills of empathy?

_____

2. In what way can you use the knowledge to improve your relationship with friends, families, colleagues and bosses?

_____

3. How can you stay nonjudgmental in the face of faults?

_____

Actions

3. Learn the skills of empathy and use them to effectively build healthy relationships and environments.

• **Checklist**

1. Shame is universal, Empathy is learnable as well as teachable. That's encouraging.

CHAPTER FIVE

WHO WE ARE IS HOW WE LEAD

Most of us are used to self-protection mechanism because of the environment we grew up in. In some cases, our parents were the ones who taught us these mechanisms, they taught us that our only defense was to armor up. The armors we wore became our only armor, a protective shield from the disappointment, the pain and hurt around us. And despite how many years have passed since, we still wear this armor taught to us by our parents who themselves lack confidence in themselves as indi viduals and as parents. Some of us go on to pass it unto our own children and so on and so forth. This way, the world would remain broken. But if we can learn to open up to learning what it takes to be truly grounded in confidence of self and of others we can fix our broken world.

Here is how the author puts it, *"grounded confidence is the messy process of learning and unlearning, practicing and failing, and surviving a few misses. This brand of confidence is not blustery arrogance or posturing or built on bullshit; it's real, solid, and built on self -awareness and practice. Once we witness how courage can transform the way we lead, we can trade the heavy, suffocating armour that keeps us small for grounded confidence that lifts us up and supports our efforts to be brave."*

There is no better way to have put it. We can't always run when faced with. We need to learn how to be brave even in the face of it. This way we will be able to live into our values, build trust and rise every time we fall.

We can learn grounded confidence from the author's analogy of sportsmen and women. An average athlete, trains at least, 6 hours in a day, 6 days a week. One good example is Jessica Ennis, who was reported to have put in 10,000 hours in preparation for the 2012 London Olympic Games. 10,000 hours! This should give you an idea what it takes to practice consistently. It takes a lot of practice to build up grounded confidence. These athletes develop fundamental skills to dare greatly through disciplined practice. Leaders can also develop disciplined practice of rumbling with vulner ability. What this will do is that it will give them the strength and emotional stamina to dare greatly without wanting to run, shut down or act up in the face of shame.

Grounded Confidence = Rumble Skills + Curiosity + Practice

The saying, curiosity kills the cat has always been a saying used to caution people from looking deeper or daring greatly. This is because sometimes the people who say this to us are themselves afraid of daring. This saying by British playwright, Ben Johnson in his 1598 play, **'Every Man and his Honour'**, talks of the danger of unnecessary investigation and experimentation. But, upon the premise of the subject matter, I beg to disagree that curiosity kills the cat. On the contrary, curiosity kills ignorance. And I dare say that ignorance is one of man's greatest enemy.

In October of 2014, a study published on the journal Neuron suggests that the brain's chemistry changes when we become curious, helping us better learn and retain information. When we are curious about a subject, we begin to ask questions, questions can lead us into finding answers and there comes research, improved learning, intelligence , even creativity and problem solving. More than anything else, it is worthy of note that curiosity is a blend of vulnerability and courage.

Speaking of courage, sometimes we find ourselves in the arena, standing and facing our fears not because we are doing it for ourselves, but for our critics. This is bad. We shouldn't be in the arena rumbling with vulnerabi lity for critics' sake. We should be there for us. We should be there in the arena to rumble with vulnerability, learn and grow not because the critics are watching. One way to do that is to always remind ourselves the reason we stepped into the arena in t he first place. Even if we were driven by curiosity, we must stay aligned with our values. And when we fall during the rumble, our values should remind us why we went into the arena in the first place.

DRIVING GREATNESS FROM CURIOSITY AND LEARNING

George Lowenstein in his 1994 article, proposed that curiosity is the feeling of deprivation we experience when we identify and focus on a gap in our knowledge. This simply means that we have to have some level of knowledge or awareness before we can get curious. That is very important for us to know. We are only curious about things we are aware of. We aren't curious about things we are unaware of or know nothing about. That is how curiosity works. There must be a prior knowledge, at least something tangible... curiosity strives to fill in the gap.

PRACTICING VULNERABILITY

Show people care. Just show people you care, that's the best way to practice vulnerability. You do that by sharing your story, sharing your vulnerability (with the right people) always o pen up a channel of communication that might lead to rumbling and growth.

BECOMING SELF-AWARE

Sometimes we are not able to connect with the intentions driving our thoughts and during times like this we are unable to align with our values. This causes us to be shortsighted and sometimes take decisions without a complete diagnosis of these intentions. This is where our square squad comes in. In times like this they can give us honest and helpful feedback, one that comes from a place of love and gentlenes s. What this will do is to help us realign with our values, assess our intentions and be conscious of ourselves in our dealings. But it is also important to state that we may not always have the luxury of accessing these people on time, so it is advisable to at least, spend time in quiet reflection weekly. This will help us connect to the very intentions driving our thoughts and behaviors.

ENGAGING IN TOUGH CONVERSATIONS

Another thing that cripples relationship or even big organizations is the culture of stagnancy. They always hold on to that notion of this is the way we have always done it. And it is wrong to have such a notion. Such mentality is crippling to the growth of an organization. It hampers team growth and stifles creativity. The question to ask people who hold on to such notion or mentality is, "how much progress have you made so far and at what cost?"

To be candid, the fact that something has always been in a particular way doesn't mean it can't or shouldn't be changed. And, in all honesty, we must have tough conversations sometimes to address them and bring these issues to the fore front. But we should be well aware that conversations like this are always emotionally charged and we must be prepared to engage in it. Don't shy away from it, that doesn't help matters too. Go in and rumble.

CHAPTER ANALYSIS

I think one of the most tasking jobs is being a parent. Raising children is a very difficult and yet delicate thing to do, because it will go a long way on how they would turn out in life. It will also determine how they would perceive the society before t hem. It is very important to state that, the way children are raised, is always reflective on their confidence level. And as the author made clear in this section, confidence is not some arrogance masqueraded as such. It is in being self-aware and recognizing and rumbling with vulnerability, as well as being and staying curios.

Lesson

1. Parenting is a reflection. How we parent is largely dependent on how we were raised.

2. Learning is the only truee way to become better and build healthier relationships.

3. Being courageous doesn't translate as being arrogant and rude. It is built on self-awareness.

4. Being curios can change the way we lead.

5. To be courageous, it takes constant practice and learning.

Issues Surrounding the Subject Matter.

1. How do we raise our kids?

_____

Is it as a result of how we were raised ourselves, or as a result of how we have come to view the world through our experiences   even   as   adults?
_____

2. Is curiosity not a dangerous thing, especially when it involves   dealing   with   emotions?
_____

<u>Goals</u>

3. How do you recognize arrogance when it is masked as confidence?

    _____

4. How can you constantly practice to be confident, when it gets exhausting?
    _____

5. How will you deal with issues at the workplace that involves a status quo, a long age culture stifling productivity and growth?

    _____

6. How do you stay self-aware in the midst of doubts while rumbling with vulnerability?

_____

Actions

1. Try to learn through practice, rumbling and curiosity.

Checklist

1. Confidence is built over a long period of practicing, over exposing yourself to the blows of the arena. Confidence takes time, give yourself time.

PART TWO
CHAPTER SIX

DARING LEADERS WHO LIVE INTO THEIR VALUES ARE NEVER SILENT ABOUT HARD THINGS.

There comes a point in one 's life that their faces are buried deep in the mud, their heads filled with shame and all they want to do is bolt out the door. In times like this when they are covered with shame in the arena, times when all they want is to breathe properly, the voices of critics are usually the loudest and they might easily forget their values. Moments like this are suffocating and the voices of the critics might dr own our values and reasons why we were in the arena in the first place. This is how the author put it, *"In those tough matches, when the critics are being extra loud and rowdy, it's easy to start hustling—to try to prove, perfect, perform, and please."* It is important to remember why we are in there. Else, they will get to our heads and our effort would most likely be a wasted one. As the author further explains, *"In those moments when we start putting other voices in front of our own, we forget what made us go into the arena in the first place, the reason we're there."*

We should also know that sometimes it is best to not enter some kinds of tough conversation. It doesn't mean I am saying we shouldn't step into the arena and rumble with our vulnerability. But we must understand that some tough conversation shouldn't have to happen. And if at all we enter those conversations, we shouldn't enter empty handed. Daring leaders never enter conversations completely empty handed —they always carry with them, the clar ity of value.

Speaking of values, the Oxford English Dictionary, define values as "principles or standards of behavior; one's judgment of what is important in life." As interesting as that is, the author's definition is simpler and easier to assimilate:

"A value is a way of being or believing that which we hold most important. Living into our values means that we do more than profess our values, we practice them. We walk our talk —we are clear about what we believe and hold important, and we take care that our intentions, words, thoughts, and behaviors align with those beliefs."

HOW DO WE DO THAT?

Step One: We Can't Live Into Values That We Can't Name

The things we hold dear, the things which are important in our lives should be clearly defined. This way we will be able to stay true to our values. Also, some people separate or create a fine but problematic distinction between their values at work and that at home. Our values should be one and the same, be it at the place of work or home.

For clarity sake, make a list of your core values and narrow it down to two. The thing about core values is this, they help in driving your courage to stay in the arena, to have that conversation you will rather not have. What this means is that it will help you choose courage over your comfort and that builds integrity. Values are meant to be practiced not just to profess it.

Courage is also, finding the power to let go of hurtful things said to you. You should feel a deep resonance of self -identification. And to do that, you can ask yourself the following questions:

1. Does this define me?

2. Is this who I am at my best?

3. Is this a filter that I use to make hard decisions?

Step Two: Taking Values from BS to Behaviour

Many of us know a lot of people who profess value but never practice it. It is one of the reasons why a button is switched off in us when some people start talking about value. The author explains that this doesn't just happen to individuals, it happens to organizations too. Only 10 percent of the organizations which profess values actually create enabling environment that add these values and demand accountability.

In her words, *"only ten percent of organizations have operationalized their values into tea chable and observable behaviors that are used to train their employees and hold them accountable."*

For us to stay true to our values, we can define three to four behaviours that support them and three to four actions we are often tempted to do which are o pposites of our values. If we can do this, we can easily identify the things, thoughts or actions preventing us from showing up when we should. They will also help us to not shame people, blame or hate them but to only hold them accountable.

Value #1 _____

1. What are three behaviours that support your value?

2. What are three slippery behaviours that are outside your value?

3. What's an example of a time when you were fully living into this value?

Value #2 _____

1. What are three behaviours that support your value?

2. What are three slippery behaviours that are outside your value?

3. What's an example of a time when you were fully living into this value?

Step Three: Empathy and Self-Compassion: The Two Most Important Seats

Theodore Roosevelt's 'Citizen in a Republic' speech as said at the beginning of the book, is one speech which has inspired generations. Despite how long ago, every line still rings true. One line we should never fo rget is this, '*It is not the critic who counts...* ' This is because when we are in the arena of life, be it marriage, academics, career, business or even faith, the voices of critics and cynics are usually the loudest.

At times like this we should learn to not focus on those voices telling us we are not enough, or who the hell we think we are, or the eyebrows who looked down on us from their noses especially when we have a stand on issues like gender, race, and sexual orientation, physical or cognitive abilit y. Focus on those voices cheering you on and strengthening your values.

When we face the gremlins, when their voices are amplified and our face down on the mud, we are almost tempted to keep silent and retreat. But silence is not courage, nor is it a comp onent of brave culture. Silence is not brave leadership. And no matter how emotionally charged it is, as brave leaders we should never ignore difficult conversations. Yes, it is true that conversations like racial, sexual, class and gender conversations ar e difficult to have, we should not shy away from it. First off, we must understand we are different, different experience, different history. Secondly, we must note that we can never completely predetermine the outcome of these conversations. And lastly, we don't have to go into the conversation armed with all the answers. It is okay not to know orbe someone who can facilitate an error free discussion on hard topics.

Here is how the author puts it, *"someone who says I see you. I hear you. I don't have all the answers, but I'm going to keep listening and asking quest ions."*

We all have the capacity to do that. When we do this, we will leave no room for secrecy and silence empowered by intimidation or fear and judgement. This way we will eradicate fear from the workplace. And as the author right lee said, in the whole arena only two seats matters the most. One for empathy and the other for self -compassion. The empathy seats should be occupied by people who know our value and helps us to put them into actions and the self -compassion seat should be occupied by us.

These are the questions we should ask ourselves:

1. Who is someone who knows your values and supports your efforts to live into them?

2. What does support from this person look like?

3. What can you do as an act of self -compassion to support yourself in the hard work of living into your values?

4. What are the early warning indicators or signs that you're living outside your values?

5. What does it feel like when you're living into your values?

6. How does living into your two key values shape the way you give and receive feedbac k?

Living into Our Values and Feedback

One of the biggest challenges we face at work as stated by the author, is staying aligned with our values when giving and receiving feedback. The question now is, how do we give feedback and still stay aligned to our values?

The following will serve as pointers:

1. I know I'm ready to give feedback when I'm ready to sit next to you rather than across from you.

This shows that we are eliminating every power, class and difference. We are creating a bond that tell s the other person, they can trust us with their vulnerability.

2. I know I'm ready to give feedback when I'm willing to put the problem in front of us rather than between us (or sliding it toward you).

We usually find it hard sometimes to give feedback . This is because we find ourselves putting out the problems or someone's own faults when they share with us. I know I am ready to give feedback when I can look beyond your faults, see your intents, understand your process and simply be on your side.

3. I know I'm ready to give feedback when I'm ready to listen, ask questions, and accept that I may not fully understand the issue.

Have you not noticed that we sometimes make it harder for people whom we are trying to be there for? We do this when we come into conversation acting as though we have all the answers. Especially as leaders, during feedback sessions, we most times forget that we should be facilitating, instead we move into lecturing. When we do this, our goal is to round it all up. But when we come from a place of curiosity and acceptance that we may not have all the answers, we will be able to give better feedbacks.

4. I know I'm ready to give feedback when I'm ready to acknowledge what you do well instead of just picking apart your mistakes.

This is important, especially when we have a deadline to meet as leaders. It is usually hard to not point to the faults and mistakes. Daring leaders, however, focuses on giving feedbacks that will boost their team's strengths and help them in working on the mistakes.

5. I know I'm ready to give feedback when I recognize your strengths and how you can use them to address your

challenges.

The author was right when she said, "I believe a strengths-based feedback style is the best approach, in which you expl ain some of the strengths or things that they do really well that have not been applied to the current situation."

6. I know I'm ready to give feedback when I can hold you accountable without shaming or blaming.

It is a sad thing to admit it, but it is true what the author said, "Many of us were raised in families where feedback came in only one of two packages —shame or blame." So, many of us never learnt the skill of productive and respectful feedback. The happy thing is, this skill can be learnt.

7. I know I'm ready to give feedback when I'm open to owning my part.

We need to come to a place where we acknowledge our own faults and wrongs in a matter so we can give productive and respectful feedbacks.

8. I know I'm ready to give feedback when I can genuinely thank someone for their efforts rather than just criticizing

them for their failings.

Let not criticism be the first earn of action and let it never be any line of action. Look for the opportunity to point them to the good they did or what they got right.

9. I know I'm ready to give feedback when I can talk about how resolving these challenges will lead to growth and opportunity.

As a leader, it is important to understand that you are responsible for your team and also responsible for the organization. Therefore, when you notice something needs to be change d, be ready to discuss it, but in a productive and respectful manner .

10. I know I'm ready to give feedback when I can model the vulnerability and openness that I expect to see from you.

As leaders, it is important to know that we must ourselves model vulnerability first before we demand it from others. We can't expect people to be vulnerable with us when we are all armoured up ourselves. Therefore, we must practice vulnerability in order to encourage openness, trust, curiosity and even questions.

Lastly, as leaders, we must learn to allow people have feelings without taking responsibility for those feelings. Make space for people to feel the way they want to, don't push them for having those feelings or try to take responsibility for them. No. That's not your job.

GETTING GOOD AT RECEIVING FEEDBACK

People are always ready to give you their feedback, regardless of how harsh it comes across to you. It is the times that we are in. Everybody's got an opinion about something and everything, and even about you. From birth, we have been receiving feedbacks, from parents to teachers, to clergy, coaches, college professors, colleagues, managers, spouses and bosses.

Therefore, we must learn how to take feedbacks, regardless of how it comes across. However, the questions we should ask ourselves are, how do we stay aligned with our values while receiving feedbacks? How can we take these feedbacks and turn it into learning?

Receiving feedback is a skill that is learnable. It takes constant practice to be able to receive feedback and avoid being defensive about it or formulate responses immediately.

KNOW MY VALUES = KNOW ME. NO VALUES= NO ME.

We should learn how to share values in order to build trust. It is one thing that daring leaders know and practice. When we share our own stories we help others to see clearly and understand their own journey. But, the problem is, leaders often shy away from telling their stories. Sometimes when they do, their team cannot connect to it. The reason for this isn't far-fetched. Their stories are either false, spiced or sometimes unreal. This affects connectivity.

When we share real and genuine stories, we connect to others. This is because there is something in it that rings true. We may be working or even living with people for years without knowing some things about them, things we should know. But because there is no culture of value sharing and rumbling with vulnerability, we wouldn't know. You will be shocked what you will find out about your colleagues, and even sometimes your siblings and even your spouse.

CHAPTER ANALYSIS

The author used this section to give us a clear picture of how hard it is to see through some conversations and experiences and reminded us that it is always darkest before dawn. Beyond that, it shows us the necessity of value, how to receive and give feedback. The author achieved a whole lot with this chapter.

Lesson

1. It is tougher before it gets better especially when it comes to vulnerability.

2. It helps to remember our values when we are in the arena, else, the voices of critics and cynics will push us to run away from the arena.

3. Narrowing down our values to the most vital ones helps to lean on them in those faced down moments in the ring.

4. Don't just talk about value, practice it, especially at the workplace.

5. Recognizing those behaviors that strengthen my value and those that I am tempted to run to when I am feeling uncertain, threatened or faced down.

6. Understanding that giving and receiving feedback is a skill, one that is both teachable and learnable.

Issues Surrounding the Subject Matter.

1. How do we lean on our values and not hold on to hurt?

_____

2. How do we truly share values and maintain connections in workplaces?

_____

–

3. Giving and receiving feedback are equally difficult. How do we understand how to give feedback to someone or a team mate who is overly defensive?

   _____

   –

Goals

1. How do you focus on self-compassion when you're hurt?

   _____

2. Having learnt how to know when to give feedback, how can you apply it to become a daring leader?

   _____

3. Who are the people that knows your value and how can you get them to support you?

   _____

Actions

1. Try to learn how to lean on to your values and focus on the people who help you.

2. In the face of feedback, criticism, lean on self - compassion and your values.

Checklist

1. Self-compassion should be something you pay close attention to. Always show your self kindness, love and gentleness.

PART THREE

CHAPTER SEVEN

BRAVING TRUST

INTEGRITY IS CHOOSING COURAGE OVER COMFORT

This part started with so many stories and it helped us to see that it is hard to build trust especially at the workplace.

Trust Talk We Can Actually Hear

When talking about trust, don't beat about the bush. Be bullet specific. Let people know exactly what you are talking about. Point out specific behaviours, and where the problem lies so it can be worked on.

According to the author, there are seven behavio urs that make up the anatomy of trust. And all captured in the word, BRAVNG.

The BRAVING Inventory

- Boundaries: Though we talk about sharing values and building trust, we should learn the place of boundaries. Respect people's boundaries and make sure they respect your own boundaries.

- Reliability is something that is lacking in this age and time. When we say we will do something, fulfil a task or meet up a deadline, we never really do them. Reliability will play a huge role in how people perceive you. How do you do this? Stay away from your competencies and limitations, so you won't make promises you can't keep.

- Aaccountability : Blame shifting is something that is digging deep into relationships, careers and even businesses. When we earn to own up our m istakes, apologize and make amends, it shows how accountable we are.

- Vault: What is not yours to share, don't share. Especially when it doesn't even you. This alone kills team spirit in workplaces. When you're trusted with an information, keep it. Lock it up in a vault.

- Integrity: This is simply doing more than just the talk, it is working the work. Which is to say that, you are practicing what you professed? It is choosing courage over one's personal comfort and choosing what is right over what is fun.

- Non-judgment: Your ability to look at things objectively, to look beyond right or wrong and focus on perception and intent.

- Generosity: Being generous is you giving the kindest and bravest of interpretation of to the other person's intention, words and actions.

The BRAVING acronym shows that it takes real courage and bravery to do these things. It is surprising how many of us run with the misconception that gossiping or divulging of secrets improves or solidifies relationships. It is really surprising.

Gossiping or divulging of secrets does not improve relationships in anyway, especially at the workplace. The only thing it does is to create an artificial connection. Things like this make the other person trust us even less.

Trust on the other hand, as defined by the author, is the stacking of small moments over time. Moments when you're not betraying the other person's trust, nor the trust of someone not present in the room at the moment. Trust is respect and honor. It is something that is built over time, it can't be summoned, demanded or commanded.

THE BASICS OF SELF TRUST

Trust is relational. Trust can't truly stand alone on its own. It is in practice with others that trust is built. However, the core foundation of trust is in our ability to trust ourselves.

Trusting ourselves can be a problem, especially when we have been betrayed and hurt in the past. Experiences that shattered not just our trust in people but in ourselves makes it very difficult for us to step into the future open minded. As humans, there is no escaping it. At one point in our lives, we have or we will experience betrayal. This can be a major setback to trusting people or even trusting ourselves.

However, we can find answers by asking questions, using the BRAVING inventory as a yardstick to measure and understand what happened. Also, let this be a guide in dealing with people in future.

Ask yourself if you respected your own boundaries in the situation. Could you have counted on yourself? Did you hold yourself accountable or did you blame o thers? Did I share what is not mine to share, or did I allow others share with me what they had no business sharing? Did I choose courage over comfort? Was I judgemental with myself? And finally was I generous towards myself?

CHAPTER ANALYSIS

There are so many takeaways from this section, but the most significant is courage. The courage to become daring leaders lies solely on our ability to look past our own comfort, to step in and have those difficult conversations that create spaces for trustworthiness, growth and real connection.

Lesson

1. Integrity is being courageous instead of being comfortable.

2. Avoiding conversations no matter how difficult will never solve anything.

3. We should learn how to set boundaries both for ourselves and for others.

4. Being reliable will improve a relationship than doing a reliable job.

5. More than anything, self-trust is the core foundation of building trust.

Issues Surrounding the Subject Matter.

1. How do we get specifics on behaviours crippling growth and still avoid hurting others?

_____

2. Can we keep from sharing what isn't ours to share when not keeping it is harmful to the organization?

_____

3. How do we keep from being ungenerous with others who have treated us so badly in the past?

_____

–

Goals

1. How can you put the BRAVING inventory to good use?

_____

2. How do you hold yourself accountable?

_____

3. How do you build your own self trust?

_____

Actions

1. Try to build your integrit y by being accountable to yourself and to others, as well as reliable and generous as well.

<u>Checklist</u>

1. Treat others the way you treat yourself, treat yourself the way you treat others. Be accountable, be reliable.

PART FOUR

CHAPTER EIGHT

LEARNING TO RISE

We live in a culture that celebrates winning and frowns against failing. To some extent this stifles growth. I am not saying we should celebrate failures. No. What I am saying is this, failing should be taught to people, especially in an organization. Sometimes we learn far more from failure than from success. Any organization which gives room for failure encourages creativity. However, most organizations put up a perfectionism standard that stifles the growth of its workers. Their workers live in fear of failure, being sacked or put on probation, therefore, risks are not being taken and creativity not encouraged.

The Reckoning, the Rumble, the Revolution

I get it that organizations are scared of giving room for failure because they are afraid that people would abuse it. But it is important people learn to fail in order to encourage creativity. However, despite teaching how to fail and creativity goes hand in hand, we should also teach how to rise. The point of falling is to rise. A child learning how to walk must first learn how to fall and stand up over and over again. Even as adults, we fall while walking sometimes. But lessons from childhood make us stand immediately.

The author was particular about learning to Rise in this part of the book. Because sometimes it is comfortable to remain where we are and blame everything for our failure. We need to learn how to rise up from the mud of our falls, live past our mistakes by overcoming them and finally facing and dealing with our hurts from those failures in a way that helps to grow from it. The reward of rising past our failures is enormous. She puts it this way, *"When we have the courage to walk into our story and own it, we get to write the ending. And when we don't own our stories of failure, setbacks, and hurt — they own us."*

THE RECKONING

Most of the time when things happen to us we are often overwhelmed by emotions. And when our emotions take over, we find it hard to think things through. It is no fault of o urs, it is how we are wired. We are emotional beings. We may think and reflect on them later on the things we would have done differently. But the ability to recognize when something is happening to us, see how they triggered our emotions, is something that rising leaders do. If we can learn this, it will help us in becoming good leaders and help those we are leading. We shouldn't be like most people who are afraid of failing and therefore opt for the easier way by offloading on others.

The author gave six strategies on how these people do it. Here are they:

Strategy #1: Chandeliering

People do this a lot. This is simply unleashing or exploding a pent up emotion on people you feel comfortable with or who are your subordinates, in a way that you will nev er do in the presence of the people you want t o impress or influence.

Offloading Strategy #2: Bouncing Hurt

Ego is an enemy with many other friends. But the dangerous thing is that ego always comes as a friend to us whenever we feel hurt or shame. The ego steps in to protect us from feeling that way and with it comes its friends. Most times anger and blame are t he two friends that comes with ego. And it readily offers them to us in exchange for our hurt. So, instead of feeling hurt, we find ourselves feeling angry, throwing blames and making excuses just to self-protect.

Offloading Strategy #3: Numbing Hurt

Often times when we say we feel numb, it is assumed that we don't feel anything at all. On the contrary, in order to self-protect, we can offload emotions through getting numb.

Offloading Strategy #4: Stockpiling Hurt

This is packing down the pain, and in stead of unleashing it on others, we keep gathering these pains until our bodies can't take it no more.

Offloading Strategy #5: The Umbridge

There are people who come off to us as perfect, people who never have bad days and never face hard times. Often times when we relate with them we find it hard to trust them. This is because we know that life is a two edged sword, there are days of happiness and there are days of sadness. When we talk to people who go about like there are no worries in the world, we find it hard to develop connection with them because they appear false and unreal.

Offloading Strategy #6: Hurt and the Fear of High - Cantering

We mostly deny or refuse to acknowledge how we feel because of the fear of getting trapped in it. Trapped in a position that does not allow us to go forward or backward. This is another way of self-protection. Because we want to keep things under control and not lose it.

STRATEGIES FOR RECKONING WITH EMOTION

In contrast to the above strategies used by people to dump their feelings on others and be comfortable doing so, we can use box breathing method to get over how we feel in those moments of hurt and shame. See the following:

1. Inhale deeply through your nose, expanding your stomach, for a count of four.

2. Hold in that breath for a count of four.

3. Slowly exhale all the air through your mouth, contracting your stomach, for a count of four.

4. Hold the empty breath for a count of four

Also when we take a step back and ask ourselves some questions, our reaction to things might be a lot better and different. Ask yourself questions like:

1. Do I have enough information to freak out about this situation?

2. If I do have enough data, will freaking out help?

This kind of questions helps inform a better decision.

The Rumble: Conspiracies, Confabulations, and Shitty First Drafts

I like what the author said about this, *if the reckoning is how we walk into a tough story, the rumble is where we go to the mat with it and own it.* And this phrase, *in the absence of data, we will always make up stories* explains a lot about how the human mind works. We shouldn't choose the comfort of not knowing over pressing to know. Professional writers understand something that most people don't and that is what they call it the *shitty first draft.* They know that the first draft is always a shitty draft, a draft that we just type away. We have to revisit it and edit and rewrite to make it polished and ready.

In the same way, the first sets of stories we tell ourselves when faced with fears and insecurities, are similar to that. We make up worst case scenarios, and our emotions helps to drive it home by making us feel like that is all that there is to it all. It is all a shitty first draft, edit your thoughts and rewrite it. Confabulation on the other hand, is that lie we tell ourselves in the absence of any information or a gap in story.

When faced with all these, we should rumble our questions with the following:

1. What more do I need to learn and understand about the situation? What do I know objectively? What assumptions am I making?

2. What more do I need to learn and understand about the other people in the story? What additional information do I need? What questions or clarifications might help?

3. What more do I need to learn and understand about myself?

THE DELTA

The Delta is us walking in our own truth, walking in our own stories. This sets the difference between the truth we learnt during rumbling and what we make up about our experience.

The revolution

What is success to you? Is what you call success determined by societal standards or measured by the requirements of others? Or is success what you say it is? I think personally, we should be able to define what success means to us in order to avoid unnecessary pressure. This last part of the book, is about us starting the revolution of rumbling, of learning, overcoming our mistakes and understanding that it is a lifelong process that will serve as filters for our choices and daring to lead. The author wants us to ask ourselves every step of the way, if our choices are what bring us joy and meaning to our lives, stir up courage even if it means rumbling in the Arena. This is the revolution with self and with the rest of the world.

CHAPTER ANALYSIS

This is a revolutionary chapter, a beautiful way to drive home the point before the conclusion. It is full of encouraging and valuable lessons, especially in dealing with people.

Lesson

1. There is shame in failing, but shame isn't a finality of result, nor a definition of who we are.

2. We can always rise up from any failure whatsoever.

3. Who should always decide how the narrative goes, step in and own our story and give it the kind of ending we want it to have.

4. To avoid offloading how we feel on others.

5. Learnt the strategies of dealing with our emotions and feelings.

Issues Surrounding the Subject Matter.

1. Some failures can so cripple us we find it hard to rise again. How do we learn to rise from such?

   _____

2. What does it mean to rise to become a daring leader?

_____

3. How do I do away with shitty first draft stories when in the arena?

_____

–

4. Revolution is an interesting word, to actually start is a daunting task. How do I?

_____

–

Goals

1. How will you avoid offloading emotions on people, even when it feels as though they deserved it?

_____

2. How do you avoid going numb when the rumbling gets too tough?

_____

3. How do you stop yourself from stockpiling emotions and putting your body under undue harm?

_____

4. How can you use the skills learnt from the strategies of reckoning with emotions to drive meaningful, productive and Non-judgmental conversation at home or at the workplace?

_____

Actions

1. Always discard the shitty first draft of a story, that first sets of voices that tells you, you are not good enough or who do you think you are.

2. Try to always step in, own your story and give it the ending you desire.

Checklist

1. The revolution is here, the revolution is now and the revolution begins with us

<u>CONCLUSION</u>

This book is a revolutionary book, a book about leadership. It is a powerful book not because it is on how to lead people, but on how to lead oneself. Unlike other books, it focuses on the things that happens within more than the things that happened without. This is because if only we can start learning how to control the things within, when external influences come at us, we would have built enough emotional stamina to stand it and shoulder the weight of their impacts. This is a book on leaders who dare to lead not from a place of perfectionism and self -protection but from a place of vulnerability, self -awareness, trust and the ability to create spaces that do not stifle growth but encourage others.

In this book, one would discover that vulnerability is not the same thing as weakness, but a path way to strength. This book is one that readers would learn a lot from. It doesn't matter if readers are familiar with the authors work before now, this book is packed enough to teach them how to be daring leaders revolutionizing the workplace by learning how to be vulnerable and honest.

Finally, to be able to lead others successfully, we must first learn to attain success leading ourselves.

CPSIA information can be obtained
at www.ICGtesting.com
Printed in the USA
BVHW041401020221
599230BV00022B/1144

9 781953 857026